To Wendy—
I'm always excited to share words with you, whether it be poetry or conversation. So glad you moved to Maine!
—Suzanne

BRIGHT
GLINT
GONE

Poems by
Suzanne Langlois

Suzanne L...

Maine Chapbook Series
Selected by Martha Collins

Maine Writers & Publishers Alliance
2020

ISBN: 978-1-7356732-0-2

©2020
Published in the United States of America
by the Maine Writers & Publishers Alliance
Portland, Maine

Publication made possible by grants from the Maine Arts Commission
and the Margaret E. Burnham Charitable Trust.

Cover Art by Douglas W. Milliken
Copy Editing by Hannah Perry

Book Design & Editing by Pink Eraser Press

to my dad, who taught me to love words

TABLE OF CONTENTS

INTRODUCTION

by Martha Collins

Reading through *Bright Glint Gone* for the first time, I was delighted by the poet's unexpected ways of perceiving the familiar, her stunning metaphors and turns of phrase, her delicate balance of humor and wisdom. The pleasure only deepens on rereading.

In poem after poem, Suzanne Langlois surprises. She depicts herself as a turtle in one poem, as a coyote ("I look down / at my arms and they are legs") in another. "The Wheel of Fortune" has a flat tire, an ended relationship begins "He mistook me for a getaway car," and an early spring is only "half out of her clothes, rolling / a stocking slowly down her leg."

These transformations and extended metaphors are a source of delight and even laughter, but they are conduits for more. The speaker is explicitly and often contentedly without a partner in many of the poems, "reveling in the joy of keeping / myself to myself." But loss and grief underlie the collection, and give the poet license to offer mature and hard-earned wisdom, often in aphoristic one-liners.

The voice is sure of itself, a seamless blend of colloquial familiarity and rhetorical care that will keep you alert and connected. By the final poem, you'll feel as if you've met a delightful new friend and are cheering her on as she "passes through" to whatever experience awaits her.

SELF-PORTRAIT AS A TURTLE

I would invite you inside
but there is no room in here,
even for me, which is why
my arms, legs, head, and tail
are all hanging out the windows.
I do not contain multitudes.
I barely contain a single 'tude.
I sit here like a bump on a log,
but I am not a bump on a log—
I'm a disembodied bump,
a nomadic bump looking for
a place to rest my bone home.
When I find one, I hunker
down for a while, become
my own bunker until I have
to move again. When I do,
I plod and lurch, a stiff geriatric.
I'm slow as tree sap, but I live
a long time and am comfortable
in mud—more comfortable than
lumbering around out here,
anyway, looking awkward
and conspicuous and most likely
not worth the effort required
to get inside, at least not if
the visible bits are any guide,
a question even I can't answer
having never gotten far enough
outside myself to see myself.
I'd like to invite you inside

just so you could describe
me to myself, so I can finally
know who it is I live with,
but when there's space
for another soul in this shell
it will be because I'm
no longer here.

DRINK TO THIS

shake a pair of dice
in the bottom of the wine glass
stain the tablecloth

why drink if not to gamble
if not to drop the reins
and urge the horses on

adult behavior is a conscious act
so let's drink to unconsciousness
we all take our clothing off too soon

the night starts with a flame
that fits in the palm of a hand
like a wine glass

and ends in a forest fire
so many mistakes begin
with wanting to be warm

FORTUNE

Sometimes, Luck comes incognito,
with unkempt hair and bad breath,
and so you turn her away. Sometimes
Luck is the frog you wouldn't kiss.
Sometimes Luck is a cosmic gladiator
come to fight the part of you bent
on your own destruction—
a delicate mission, like removing
a tumor the body doesn't want
to part with. How frustrated
Luck must feel when we call
what happens next bad Luck.
Luck did her best to save us from
ourselves. Luck is not to blame
for our failure to recognize her
when she knocked on the door,
when she stood on the stoop
holding her small bouquet,
ready to give us everything.

TRAFFIC

When I was a kid,
the dogs ran free,
which is why
they kept dying.

My first heartbreak
was a dog that didn't
come back. I remember
my father handing
my mother the empty collar.

This is how I learned
there are troubles so deep
you can't climb out.
There are mistakes
you only make once,
and not because
you've learned.

Still, I could not resist
the urge to chase down
whatever needed chasing—
whatever beckoned from
the far side of traffic.

So many close calls,
strange cars I climbed into
that could have turned
into a missing child poster,
an obituary—my body
discovered in a ditch.

Instead, the people who
pulled over when I flashed
my thumb all wanted
the same thing—to save me
from whoever might be
driving the next car.

They delivered me
home with a scolding
but otherwise intact,
more convinced than ever
of my own immortality,

more convinced than ever
that nothing bad was fast
enough to catch me.

UNDRESSING

I need help with the zipper on this skin
suit. I can't reach the pull and all
I want is to step out of it and drape it
over a chair while I smoke a cigarette
or light an orchard on fire. But it's just
me here, and knocking on my neighbor's
door to ask for a reason to stay in
my body seems a bit forward. I mean,
we haven't even exchanged cups
of sugar yet, or had a blowout fight
over who's been hogging the dryer.
We've both lived in this building
long enough to have raised a child
together, if by raised you mean
managed to keep it alive long enough
to send it to school so someone else
can have a go at it. But this is all
beside the point. The point is I have
an itch in the middle of my back,
right where the zipper would end
if I were wearing a strapless gown,
which I'm not, but a girl can dream,
right? A woman who once was a girl
can dream she's still a girl, right?
A sweet intoxicating thing, cherry
run through with a plastic sword.
But that skin doesn't fit me anymore.
That skin was just on loan, anyway.
That skin surely looks better
on whoever is wearing it now.

SLEEPLESS

He is a fistful of gravel thrown
at my bedroom window—a blinding
lamp left burning on the nightstand,

a hand that keeps dragging me
back from the threshold of sleep
only to dissolve the moment

my senses are crisp enough
to distinguish between a wish
and his skin against mine.

I know the sting of his name
will eventually fade, but now
it leaves me tender as a bruise,

and here it is, that trickle
of forgiveness—a frayed rope
I shouldn't reach for, but do.

My friends roll their eyes, his name
a lie they've grown tired of, a poorly
told story. Still, it fevers my tongue,

a glowing coal I keep dropping
into conversations to watch the ripples
spread as it sinks into the past—
its bright glint already gone.

WINTER MORNING

Half asleep, half frozen
in my thin nightgown,
I crouch before the stove's
open door, coaxing
the logs to take flame.
They whine as steam
escapes the wet wood,
bubbling from under the bark—
a froth of boiling sap.

Outside the window,
a blank cold—no sun yet,
just icy light running
its hands over the yard.
Hard to believe,
at this stiff unlit hour,
that the sky will ever
be anything but white
and distant.

The cold, sharp as a thorn
lodged in a cat's paw—
the bright pain of being awake—
will burn off like a fog
when the sun comes
strolling over the mountain,
like it's not even late,
like it hasn't kept us waiting,
like it knows it is
already forgiven.

COYOTE

In the dreams, I look down
at my arms and they are legs.
I do not wear clothing
but I am not naked.
My mouth opens nearly
from ear to ear and contains
no words. In the dreams,
I don't need words in my mouth
—my teeth are sharp enough
to speak for themselves,
to take what they want
without asking.

In a den somewhere a creature
sleeps and dreams her body bald.
She howls in terror and strange
sounds come from her throat—
they sound like *my God*
why have you forsaken me?
She rises to join her people
but they back away snarling
and then turn and run.
She tries to run with them
but they disappear into the trees
and she cannot catch
their scent. Her nose is deaf.

In the dreams, I leave
my bedroom through
the claw-torn screen.

I follow an anguished cry
I can hear with my nose.
It leads me to a den where
a naked woman rocks
on her haunches and howls
her aloneness. Her eyes
are wild but her body is not.
It is a trap she will die in.

The dream always ends
the same way—I wake
just as a bullet opens the body
I was wearing a moment ago.
Always, it takes a long moment
before I can move my limbs,
which are numb and stiff,
as though they belonged
to someone else. Always,
I am unable to make a sound
until I do, and then it is
never the sound I expected.

RECKLESS

I want the current that arcs
between two strangers
who have locked eyes
and won't look away until
they've pulled themselves
hand-over-hand along
the taut rope of hunger
stretched between them.

I want to drag myself
through the gutter
of a stranger's gaze.
I want to grab someone
by their wicked wicked want
or whatever naked part
they offer me.

I want to capsize my body
in rough water—soak my tongue
in a bottle of wine until it forgets
whose mouth it belongs in.
I want to taste the decay
of my own goodness—a thread
of mold in gorgonzola.

I want to toss all my rent money
in the wishing well and say
every wish out loud. Don't bother
to unlace me, just rip the seams—
I don't care if I fit back

into my packaging tomorrow—
I'm only going to throw it
all away when I'm done.

TRUISMS

A lie, no matter how many times
we tell it, is not truth. A lie
repeated is a secondhand lie.
A lie a million people believe
is a popular lie. A lie we forget
is a lie is a delusion. A lie
someone powerful wishes
were true is a well-funded lie,
not a well-founded truth.
We can't vote a lie true.
We can't overturn the truth.
The truth does not require
our support to be true.
It can hold itself up. It stands
tall before us even now,
even as we refuse to see it.

MISTAKE

He mistook me for a getaway car—
highway laid out
before the gleaming hood,
straight and faithful as a church aisle.

I mistook him for a muddy riverbed—
a soft thing to drift into,
something that does not grasp or let go,
just gathers itself around you.

He mistook my sigh for a promise,
a holy thing—half prayer, half spell.
He mistook me for someone
with the kind of magic
to bind what is unbound
and make it love its bonds.

I mistook his fantasy for a future
soaked in a broth of wishes—
like waking up into the incredible
dream instead of out of it,
all the disappointments undone.

He mistook my glance for an unlocked door.
I mistook his for an open window.

Now, we both know better,
and have given back the things we mistook,
but it clings to our fingers—
this stain of taking what wasn't ours,

what did not exist until we took it,
and not even then.

ANIMAL LOGIC

To a cat, the dark circle on the birdhouse
is a miracle: a hole two sparrows
disappear into and six exit, a throat
that can neither sing nor swallow.

A cat does not ask or pray—
it waits, and then takes what it wants.
A dog prays and takes what it can get—
the dead rat with its bare tail,
stiff as a candlewick.

A cat knows the length of a dog's tether
better than the dog does. A dog knows
the border of its world by the jolt of it.

A hawk that hunts under clouds
eats better than one that hunts under the sun.
Its god has no shadow, and moves
through the grey sky on grey wings.

The god of field mice is a field mouse
and prefers bright light, or else darkness,
thick as a rind—to have a shadow,
or better, to be a shadow.

A swallow's wings are spoked
with the thinnest bones, easily snapped
by a cat's paw or a hawk's talons.
Still, it carves the air with them,
slices the clouds from the sky.

A tortoise is a refugee that takes
its house with it. It doesn't know
whether it is always home or
never home. It moves slowly,
lost in this thought.

THE WHEEL OF FORTUNE

is flat and I don't have a jack
or a tire iron, or a clue how to use
one except maybe to kill a man

but it keeps spinning anyway
all wobbly and with that *thwump*
thwump of a thing that should
be round but isn't

and the people passing me
are gesturing wildly out
their windows and I just
wave back

gripping the wheel like the stem
of a wine glass or a penis I don't
know how to operate, and I'd like
to buy a vowel

whichever one will allow me
the longest uninterrupted scream
I'd like to spin again and again
until it's time to go back

to my dressing room, wipe off
my eyebrows, shuck this girdle,
and pour a glass of whatever
will blur the letters

into a puddle of spilled ambition,
and think about how I got here,
what series of accidents led
to these high heels,

this vacant smile, this shiny
new car spinning on its lazy Susan,
glittering and depreciating
by the second,

its hubcaps gleaming under
the studio lights, begging
take me, take me, I am yours
for the taking

THAW

The fern unrolls its delicate scroll,
whispering green into the breeze's ear.
The lily of the valley hangs its pale face
in supplication, and pussy willows lift
their tiny feet and paw the wind.
Everything teeters on the edge of ripening.
Soon, summer's breath will be a lagoon,
a sweaty palm clamped on the back
of the neck. Cattails will raise their
distaffs overhead, neat fists of fiber
held aloft. But for now, spring is only
half out of her clothes, rolling
a stocking slowly down her leg.

FACT CHECK

Your facts are useful, and yet, they are not my dwelling…
—Walt Whitman

My heart refuses to live in my heart,
refuses to live in the fact of my body.
It keeps flying the coop with its bumble
bee wings. Each day, my heart lifts a body
too heavy for its strength, a body so
in love with gravity, it weighs three times
what it weighs. Weight is both a number and
a value. A number is a fact that builds
a fence around a space and says no one
can enter and no one can leave, but
my heart is a burrowing creature. It has
tunneled out of more prisons than it's been
confined to, which should be impossible,
but my heart will not dwell in the possible.

PARCHED

The wind swallows its words,
decides it has nothing more
to say and suddenly every tree
forgets how to dance. The clouds
stand still in the sky until the sun
licks the moisture from their skin.
Soon the land is baked clay, quiet
as only the ghostless are quiet.
Tomorrow stays home—no reason
to drag itself from east to west,
east and west scorched to stillness,
doomsday squatting on the horizon,
sharpening its blade on a stone.

NOT A PRAYER

I've never prayed to someone or something,
only for someone or something.

If I'm going to be honest, which I haven't yet
decided, I'm not sure

whether it's that I've never believed anyone
would willingly give me what I wanted—

actually, I'm sure it's that. To ask is to give
someone power over you

or to make them aware of the power they already have,
and that never ends well. Knowing

I have power over someone makes them repulsive
to me. I don't know whether it's that

it makes them seem weak or if it's that it makes me
feel too strong. Actually, it's the second.

I know I am clumsy. I know I am bound to drop
the fragile vase, better not pick it up to begin with.

Please don't ask me what I want. That's not a prayer.
It's a polite command.

It's all you're going to get from me.

HAUNTED

There are three ghosts outside my window,
maple trees I voted to remove to make more
room for the cars in the parking lot. Five humans
could not agree on the borders between their
shared inconvenience, and since the trees
could not vote on the matter, the trees are gone,
just like that, and I cannot change my mind
and bring them back. Already they are smoke
rising from a chimney. Already they've been
converted into someone else's comfort. People
are voted out of existence every day, and every
day I cast my careless ballot when I nudge my car
into the tangle of traffic, when I eat my lunch
from a plastic cup with a foil lid and then throw
them in a plastic bag in a bin that will be emptied
into a larger bin at the end of the day and again
tomorrow and and and and remorse is brittle.
It splinters under the weight of the next optional
inconvenience. I know there is a day in the future
when I will regret every optional inconvenience
I opted out of. The obligatory suffering already
felt by so many will arrive at my door with
its own key, or a crowbar, or a curtain of flame.
Already it is spidering toward me, a rumor
that wished itself true. Already, its roots snake
under the asphalt, buckling the pavement,
ready to tear the whole thing down.

ELEGY FOR A DOG

The creature I loved has been unmade.
Every part of her, down to her whiskers,
vanished from the planet.

I miss her song—the way
she'd point her muzzle at the ceiling,
turn her black lips into an O,
and pour a moan through it.

Today I learned all the things
I can do while howling.
I can stand up or lie down.
I can rock back and forth on my haunches,
tip my head back and empty my throat.

Still, the open grave in my chest
holds her body and wishes itself a cradle.
The last time I put my hands on her belly
I felt it swell with a grief about to be born,
her body a honeycomb filled with rot
—all that sweetness wasted.

I think of the words I tried to teach her:
sit, lie down, sing,
stay, stay, stay, stay.

DROUGHT

After the dust swallowed the livestock,
stole the bees from their dry hive,
peeled the green from everything—
after a thick coat of what once was farm
filled the windowsill with black grime—
that is when my great-grandfather
went out onto the porch
and loaded the shotgun.
His young son watched him
from behind the screen door
wondering what was left to kill
in this husk of a land beaten
by the wind's calloused palms.
With even the dog gone,
what was left that could still bleed?
He wondered this as he watched
his father cross the packed earth
between the house and the barn—
stood, wondering, as the shot
tore the day into before and after.
Before, when he wondered,
and after, when he knew.

SOVEREIGN

When it finally bursts from its seed, *No*
reaches for everything it can (refuse to) touch,
dark blossoms climbing a trellis, branching
and branching again, claiming their space
with layers of imbricated leaves, a garden of *No*.
Fruit ripens under the moon's chilly gaze
and *No*, you can't have any—this whole crop
is mine to waste, if that's what I want to do,
and if that's what I want to do, it's not waste.
It's just me, sipping my own small power
from a flask, reveling in the joy of keeping
myself to myself, alone in all the best ways,
alone in all the ways I've said *Yes* to.

EGGPLANT

Like the robin's egg hiding
its drab bird in a bright blue fist,
the eggplant's skin makes
a promise it can't keep.

Enamel sheen the shade all purples
hope to be when they grow up—
the color of a heart beating
at the speed of new love.

Eggplant, you bush of indigo bloat,
fruit swelling like a corpse,
blood blister about to burst—
if I could find the thing that tastes the way
you look, I would eat nothing else.

As it is, I have no idea how to turn you into
something my mouth wants to hoard.
How often I've been seduced by skin,
only to be disappointed by mealy texture
and thin flavor—not nearly as sweet as it looked.

Probably the problem lies in my cooking,
my anemic imagination, my lack of skill with spices.
Probably everything I've ever wanted
is something I have to learn how to make.

Probably the blue of the robin's egg
is a promise to no one but the bird
curled in the palm of the sky
it's about to be born into.

GRAY

Another overcast day. Alone
at home, my future feels like
a damp cellar with no door.
The only dry thing is a cat,
and she shares her dry
with me. She tucks herself
into the valley of my lap,
and I pretend I am loved
and not just warm,
and that this is enough.

Once, I was all ripeness
and hot skin—waiting
for someone to brush
against me, sticky as a burr
and as hard to dislodge.
Giddy with a new man's
name framed in my smile
for everyone to see.

The last time someone's
bare shoulder pillowed
my head was so long ago,
it feels like it might actually
have been the last time.
But every time I've given
away a piece of my solitude,
I've wanted it back
almost immediately.
I remember how I craved

an empty bed, and turned
the knuckles of my spine
toward the man I wanted
gone.

Now, age has licked
the sugar from my skin.
It tangles its fingers
in my hair and yanks
the gray down each shaft.
Time is the tongue
I will dissolve on.
My head, a pile of cinders
on the white pillowcase,
cat curled in the notch
behind my bent knees.

FOG

Driving home, the headlights press
their palms against the fog—
a blindfolded person navigating

an unfamiliar room.
This is how love feels to me,
or whatever comes before love—

the amorphous swirl churning
in the gut, not ready to name itself,
its half-existence just brushing

the skin with its whiskers, like a cat
that knows which parts of your body
it can curl into and be allowed to stay.

Imagine if this mist could grow skin,
like boiled milk cooling.
And imagine if I could let that skin be,

instead of clawing it open
with my fingernails,
trying to find the bones beneath.

Though I know better,
I always drive at a speed
the headlights can't keep up with,

as wall after solid wall of fog
approaches and then splits
to let me pass through.

SUZANNE LANGLOIS'S poems have appeared in *The Maine Review, NAILED Magazine, Cider Press Review, The Fourth River, Off The Coast, Rattle,* and on the Button Poetry channel. Her work has been nominated for Best of the Net, Independent Best American Poetry, and the Pushcart Prize. She holds a BA in English from Tufts University, an Ed.M. from the Harvard Graduate School of Education, and is currently an MFA candidate at Warren Wilson College. She lives inPortland and teaches high school English in Falmouth, Maine.

ACKNOWLEDGMENTS

Thanks to the following journals for giving these poems their first homes:

Bracken: "Drought"
(reprinted in the Deep Water column of *The Portland Press Herald*)

The Café Review: "Mistake"

Cider Press Review: "The Wheel of Fortune"

The Maine Review: "Animal Logic"

Menacing Hedge: "Voice Box" and "Gray"

NAILED: "Drink to This" and "Fog"

Off the Coast: "Elegy for a Dog"

Rattle: "Coyote"

Rust + Moth: "Math"

Ungatherable Things: A Word Portland Anthology: "Eggplant" and "Winter Morning"

Whale Road Review: "Fact Check"

Whisk(e)y Tit Journal: "Traffic"

ABOUT THE MAINE WRITERS & PUBLISHERS ALLIANCE

Founded by a group of small presses and writers, Maine Writers & Publishers Alliance (MWPA) has worked since 1975 to enrich the literary life and culture of Maine. We bring together Maine writers, editors, publishers, booksellers, and literary professionals at all stages of their careers to sharpen craft, create community, and celebrate great writing. MWPA has an active, growing membership of more than 1,400 literary professionals from all sixteen counties of the state. In 2019, the MWPA held four writing conferences and eighty-seven workshops in twenty-five locations across Maine, not to mention more than one-hundred free readings and community events. To help make all of our memberships, conferences, and workshops accessible, MWPA offered more than $23,000 in scholarships to Maine writers at all stages of their careers last year.

ABOUT THE MAINE CHAPBOOK SERIES

Between 1983 and 1999, the Maine Arts Commission published thirteen chapbooks in collaboration with a series of small Maine presses, and thereafter by the Maine Writers & Publishers Alliance, as part of the Maine Chapbook Series. Each year, a nationally known writer served as the judge and selected a manuscript for publication. In 2019, the MWPA re-started this beloved series.

PREVIOUS MAINE CHAPBOOK SERIES WINNERS

Ruth Mendelson, *;l,/*
Theodore Press, 1983
Selected by Philip Booth

Rebecca Cummings, *Kaisa Kilponen*
Coyote Love Press, 1986
Selected by George Garrett

Robert Chute, *Samuel Sails for Home*
Coyote Love Press
Selected by Charles Simic

Christopher Fahy,
One Day in the Short Happy Lie of Anna Banana
Coastwise Press, 1988
Selected by Mary McCarthy

Kenneth Rosen, *The Hebrew Lion*
Ascensius Press, 1989
Selected by Amy Clampitt

Denis Ledoux, *Mountain Dance*
Coastwise Press, 1990
Selected by Elizabeth Hardwick

Besty Sholl, *Pick a Card*
Coyote/Bark Publications, 1991
Selected by Donald Hall

John A.S. Rogers, *The Elephant on the Tracks and Other Stories*
Muse Press, 1994
Selected by David Huddle

Candice Stover, *Holding Patterns*
Muse Press, 1994
Selected by Mary Oliver

Sis Deans, *Decisions and Other Stories*
Maine Writers & Publishers Alliance, 1995
Selected by Cathie Pelletier

Peter Harris, *Blue Hallelujahs*
Maine Writers & Publishers Alliance, 1996
Selected by Roland Flint

Rhea Cote Robbins, *Wednesday's Child*
Maine Writers & Publishers Alliance, 1997
Selected by Sven Birkerts

Ellen Bryan Obed, *A Letter from the Snow*
Maine Author's Publishing, 1999
Selected by Lois Lowry